The Rough-Hewn Table

A Breakthrough Book / University of Missouri Press

The Rough-Hewn Table/Poems by Henry Carlile

Acknowledgments

Fiddlehead: "Blue Heron"
Poetry: "The Job"; "Endurances"
Choice: "Narcissus: A Notebook"
The Oregon Times: "Three Monuments"
Shenandoah: "Arrivals & Departures"
The Iowa Review: "The Turkey-Quill Nymph"
Concerning Poetry: "Three for the Predators"
Poetry Northwest: "Grandmother"; "Bittern";
    "Coot"; "Looking for Landmarks"; "Last Words"
Northwest Review: "Spider"; "The Ice Dreams"; "The Party"
The Malahat Review: "Praise for the Saints in Time of War";
    "The Wars of Ambition"; Confessions from a Journal"

I would like to thank the National Endowment for the
Arts for their generous award of a grant which enabled
me to complete many of the poems in this book. H.C.

Illustrations rendered by Merrill Cason for this edition.
ISBN 0–8262–0114–8 *paper*   ISBN 0–8262–0115–6 *cloth*
Library of Congress Catalog Number 70–167918
Printed in the United States of America

For Sandra

The Devins Poetry Award

The Rough-Hewn Table won, in manuscript,
the Devins Poetry Award for 1971. A provision
of the Award—the major prize of the Kansas City Poetry
Contests—is publication by the University of Missouri Press.

Henry Carlile's manuscript was chosen from several hundred
collections submitted anonymously by poets across the nation.

The annual Award is made possible by the generosity of
Dr. and Mrs. Edward A. Devins. Dr. Devins is former President
of the Kansas City Jewish Community Center and is a
patron of the Center's American Poets Series.

Contents

You have noticed that the truth comes into this world with two faces. One is sad with suffering, and the other laughs; but it is the same face, laughing or weeping. When people are already in despair, maybe the laughing face is better for them; and when they feel too good and are too sure of being safe, maybe the weeping face is better for them to see.—Black Elk

I

Grandmother

No one remembered when she first discovered God.
Her conversion was sudden as a slammed door.
Outside, my grandfather beat the doorjamb with his fist,
But she, God-furious, would not relent.
Shut up like an oyster on a speck of dirt
She praised God in her bedclothes,
Read the Bible like a French novel,
And dreamed each night of Christ the Saviour,
The lightning bolt of revelation forking at her
From the black cloud of her Bible,
And the godhead stirring inside her like a sick sea.

Overnight her skirts grew longer and her temper shorter,
The black buttons on her boots crept higher and higher
On legs that had never seen the light.
Whenever she rode the cable car downtown
She pulled her bonnet tight around her ears
To let no evil word hiss through,
Her eyes magnified by scripture,
Split by the seeing lens and reading lens
Which could never look together,
Beholders of two worlds: one black and one white,
Negative, censored, and unprintable,
A damned world bleached of color.

Stern as an iron stove
She drove her children off to church,
Beat their bottoms with a willow
To make them kneel like thirteen sinful sheep,
Recalcitrant, flagellant, bleating at the altar,
Pinched upright in their pews,
Reciting alphabets of sin while the preacher,
A red-faced Russian with a beard as black as God,
Gospeled from the pulpit
And the congregation flapped their tongues,
Prophesying improbable forgiveness.

But nothing ever was:
The family scattered out like rabbits
From the sawed-off shotgun of the true faith
While Grandmother rocked in the cradle of belief,
Reading and praying, reading and praying,
Copying scriptures on tiny scraps of paper
That peeped like mice or children
From every nook and cranny of the old house:
From cookie jars and table drawers and kitchen cupboards—
Even from the Bible itself, marsupial with misconceptions,
Threatening every minute to explode,
Until one day her heart did,
And we hunkered in the shadow of her death,
A bad-luck come-to-nothing family
Wrong since genesis.

Three Birds

Blue Heron

Spooky bird,
You, heron!
At ebb tide
In the flat
Mirror of
The world
There are
Two of you.

The natives call you shitepoke.
Do you know what they call you?
No. Of course not.
Preoccupied,
Professor of blennies,
Inspector of sculpins,
Old ferule-face,
Gray bird,
Standing strictly still
On one leg,
Hump-shouldered,
Shadowy,
Are you really there?

Is it from you we learn
The arts of meditation?
Your silence makes me fidget.

Kooawk! You talk
Just like an old professor,
And when you fly,
Your beak stuck out before
And your legs trailing behind,
Which end is which?

Now look at you!
Wings flapping like bedsheets,
Leaving a trail of dimples
Behind you.
Shitepoke.

Bittern

Green-footed,
Clinging to a wall of cattails,
Aiming your bill straight up,
Stretching out so thin
You're like a reed yourself,
You sway the way a reed sways
In a sudden gust of wind.

Your name is Thunderpumper.
Speckled brown, shy as smoke,
So self-effacing
Your eye is all I see
Peering from the cattails,
Yellow, watching me.
If I come closer
You'll flap into the air
And disappear
Floppy as an old hat.

At dusk I hear you
Calling to your mate
Most unromantic sounds,
A mallet whacking at a stake,
Then
Ploom-pudd'n, ploom-pudd'n,
And, worst of all,
Oong-ka-choonk!
Like a stopper pulled from a sink.

What are you trying to say?
Hearing you
The frogs and crickets hush.
In stunned silence,
As though someone had burped at table,
I see the mink with one paw raised,
The beaver blinking with myopic eyes,
Incisored like an English duke,
Twitching incredulous
Whiskers.

Coot

White-billed, red-eyed,
Nodding your head,
Gray as a parson,
What are you doing here
With all these folk?—
Fastidious mallards,
Gadwalls, canvasbacks,
And the dainty green-wing teal.
What a homely fellow!
Clucking *kuk*! *kuk*!
Like a hoarse hen,
Running across the water
On long, lobed toes,
Flapping your wings
Frantic as Peter.
Run a little faster
Or you'll sink!
Your flying habits
Are chaotic,
Your landings atrocious:
You knock your neighbors silly
Crashing like a brick
Or a football.

Why should I like you?
You're too foolish for belief
Rioting with your wife,
Cackling, spattering with water
Like a manic motorboat.

With intentions of rape
You chase her
Through the lily pads,
Scaring away the bass
I was going to cast for.
Then when I've called you
Every dirty name I know,
You're suddenly still.
You drift serenely with your mate
Making soft clucking sounds
I somehow understand,
Preening each other
In the gentlest motions
Of love.

Three for the Predators

At midnight on the riverbank,
burglars prowl sly-whiskered,
pilfering from the shallows
clams shut up like banks on Sunday,
quick-pincered crayfish,
snails coiled springtight
into a country of themselves,
fastidious fast fingers that probe,
find everything rock-bottom,
safe for those who touch
with a safecracker's old know-how.

High in the hemlock
eyes like two August moons blink down,
broad wings launch out suddenly
extending hooks to grapple in the depths
of air, of snow, for timider lives
of lesser consequence,
which know no acquittal
but that fine instinctual alacrity
of the hunted.

In the green world we carry with us
like a secret illness from a city
we've escaped,
know, too, the shadow suspended in green space,
the long head in which the flat eyes
tip like platters,
the two red crescent moons at the throat,
the long mouth's sinister grin,
and the chain-marked, snakelike body
waiting to swallow
anything that moves.

Last Words

The Disinheritance

Then I will not inherit this dream.
Trusted only with holding boards and plumb lines,
Fetching tools, I didn't help build:
Dunnage, driftwood, tarpaper roof,
Zigzag stovepipe whooing in the wind,
Bedrooms without closets, kitchen cupboardless,
Linoleum tiles curling up underfoot like burnt bacon,
Roofs and additions slanting away
In all directions toward no conclusion
But a stepfather's whimsical hammer
Banging all Sunday.

Goodbye chicken coop full of old lumber,
Cedar sinkbox intended for duck hunting
Serving time as a septic tank,
Playboy-girl plastered workshop
Hung with broken braces, toothless saws;
Goodbye weedy garden disinherited too,
Old car bodies stalled in a smog of blackberry brambles;
Goodbye back porch brimming with empty bottles,
Fruit jars inhabited by spiders.

I have come a last time to say
Nothing is ever finished, much less this mess
Resolvable only by fire or dynamite,
More shiftless than the sand dunes under it
And beyond it blossoming with lupine and verbena,
The white wart-encrusted, red-lacquered caps
Of the dazzling amanita packed with hallucinations,
And all day to the west of us the moon-crazed
Murdering sea gnawing its coastline.

Ocean View

Already the contractors and developers circle
    with transits and tape measures.
The bulldozer coughs nervously in the trees,
    wanting to get loose,
To bite down the house built however awkwardly
    with your own hands.
The deed signed away will destroy this land,
Mother and Stepfather; you who have disowned me
    have already left it,
Though you stand here haggling with realtors.

Let them fill the marsh with sand.
The heron and bittern and coot will desert
    this place as surely as we have.
In the country of snipes and mallards
    let them sell hot dogs and souvenirs;
The geese will pass here at night not stopping
    to fill the sedge flats with their gray bodies
    and oboe voices.

In winter, the wind will tug at the shopsigns
    and shuttered windows of the A-frame cottages,
The bunch grass will flatten and the sand hump
    into a beast shape moving inland,
Drifting over porches, scouring the paint
    from siding and doorsills,
Sifting through crevices—a presence
    the tiniest grain of which outwears us.

The Nightmares

If you could give them up, the indignities of childhood,
fatherless at age two (and how do you understand that?—
it booms like a big drum),
successions of violent stepfathers,
the gratuitous insult in the schoolyard at noon,
the nightmare in which you inch yourself down a long rope
into the grave of your mother's body,
if you could give them up . . .

*   *   *

The insurrection against history takes the form of beatings,
endless avenues of oppression.
This time you win and are guilty for it.
Alone, rubbing ruined knuckles in the empty alley
between the past and future,
you wake to resume a surface eloquence
beneath which the dream of murder babbles incoherently.
If you could give it up you would.

*   *   *

Sufferer! Habit unbecoming even the most pious
ritualist of an extinct religion.
How easy to cultivate your own volcano.
How gloomy.
You live in a clarity of acquired rite
like a New Yorker in smog.
Pray for subterranean upheavals to shake things up,
thunder and lightning to bring it all down.
The manic-depressive elements, shouldn't it be obvious
to anyone, are merely a projection
of your own condition.

*   *   *

These were your incentives: a bang on the nose,
a kick in the pants.
The pain was temporary—some consolation for inept defenses.
Now past thirty you still flinch,
come out swinging at every shadow.
You are Bogart sniping from the last crags,
transcendent, crashing out.
Only love can bring you down.

The Grief of Our Genitals

i

They droop like sad fuchsias from our bodies,
they stir blindly about like earthworms exposed to light,
they belong to us and yet we cannot own them,
we are attached like Siamese twins, one of whom is addicted,
we must share their insatiable appetites, their cravings,
and have no voice in the matter
but be as a master ruled by his dog.

ii

Dogs! How simple it is with them.
None of this complication:
Dogs do not need king-sized beds
lonely as deserted playfields.
Anywhere will do: lawn, sidewalk,
cemetery.
        They make love on our graves
and do not know how restlessly we sleep
with our arms full of dust
and lost opportunities.

iii

In the tropic of Cancer,
through jungles of viney pubescence,
the soldiers are marching, are marching,
each with his tiny carapace like a shield
and fierce as a Hun living off the country.
We are invaded!
At midnight no remedy for this but strong spirits
and in the cure the flaming penance.

The Job

At one point he comes simply to ask, why bother?
Wearing your look, speaking your speech,
Which of course are unknown to you,
He confronts you like an old friend, someone to trust.
When you complain, he smiles patient as father.
He sees into your deepest self, exposing the irrational
Motives for all your behavior, mildly explaining
In language even a simpleton might understand
Why if you don't live in the right place, if your name
Has so far as anyone can tell no right recognizable
Ethnic roots, if you know no one who can do you
A favor, you can be ignored forever because
So far as anyone who has anything whatsoever
To do with anything important happens to be
Concerned you don't exist except as a postmark,
Provincial, primitive, quaint, any one of a dozen or so
Epithets to be dropped at any gathering at which
Fashionable topics are exchanged like make-believe
Banknotes in a game of chance.
                              At which time
He remarks it's past midnight, it's time
He was going and goodbye and please call
It was nice seeing you again and leaves
At which point you remove the cotton from your ears
And return to that unfinished perfectly useless whatever-
It-was-you-were-about-to-do-before-he-called which lies
Where you left it, impossible, urgent and necessary
On the rough-hewn table lost among mountains and waterfalls.

II

Three Monuments

At Teddy Roosevelt's statue
grandfathers gather to talk
war, leaning on canes
in the easy attitudes
of mountain men propped up
on muskets.
                    The shadow of
Teddy Roosevelt's sword
falls across their feet.

As the cannon aims into
a blank river fog,
the flagstaff's empty halyard
bangs in a cold wind.

The mast of the *Oregon*
commemorates its absence
and the old ironclad
excuse of privilege.

Changes

The wind's white . . .

In the middle of my lecture on Roethke
he rose, black, tall and mean,
stretched his long basketball-player arms,
scratched his Afro and walked out.

Greenhouses full of roses mean little
to him; the nature he knows best
is human and not to be trusted
any more than a blizzard.

With a mind full of snow what can you feel?
You think blind, it's called survival,
you think ice whenever you see white,
or you try not to see when the vision blinds you,

because you have learned already
how too much thinking kills,
spreads like frost through your blood
and numbs a passionate heart.

I thought these things, and therefore I said
nothing: It was not my place to forgive,
but to ask that power if I could for all of us,
and Roethke, teacher, forgive me,

when I turned back to the page your words
accused me and I could not dance,
I could not dance at all.

White Student, White Teacher, Black Lit.

The middle passage hangs you up again.
Certain progressions always elude you:
like Dolphy's last refrain end-stopped

in the cold air of Berlin,
like the bird's note free as thistle-down.
Begin again,

listen closer, you can never quite touch it.
That life you distill away, what is left?
Pure, white, tasteless,

it lies—a formula, or less.
If you would learn you must return to the middle passage,
that bridge under water

insisting only that to cross it you drown.
Once there you must memorize by heart,
unlearning everything.

But remember this:
how the score was white,
the music black:

You never guessed our future was yours,
and now you have no future, no fortune.
Soul, you have no soul.

Now you will want to say you are sorry.
Do not be surprised then if someone
turning his head

smiles and pretends to listen.
So this is what it is like,
you never imagined it.

For how could you?—
you never listened.
Now we must practice.

Arrivals & Departures

i

He drops by before dinner, shaggy,
unannounced, happy as your Airedale
(which he sometimes resembles),
drinks coffee while you eat,

talks as much as he listens,
is so polite he's impolite,
says things he doesn't mean to,
is embarrassed, fidgets, eats

half his pudding, doesn't taste it
because he talks too much.
You swallow for him, think about
some time so long ago you'd forgotten,

wondering does he think *that*?
And the laurel blossoms from your brow.

ii

At your reading the reasonable clock said
iamb, iamb, while your words,
those brave irregulars, held hope of a
small space of timelessness—all we would need.

But the clock, predictable as always, had its way,
and the nice ladies.
One touching your coat sleeve
with an Ayn Rand novel caught
my camera's eye.
I was too sly.
As I pressed the shutter a hand moved,
a head nodded, the camera shook.

I left then with the blur of events
trapped in darkness behind
the blind eye of my lens,
and only your words to light me home
like distant stars or friends.

Confessions from a Journal

They buried me in a football
in a dream of interceptions.
Now I consult the one-eyed oracle
for the scoreless answer.

*   *   *

It's Mother again,
getting a new permanent
from the head herpetologist.

*   *   *

I leave the telephone off
the hook now because you
always call when I'm naked.

*   *   *

These faults record me better
than I do them.

*   *   *

Writing this fragment
I have no doubt
I chose the lesser way.

*   *   *

My words had they been
deeds might have helped me.
Now they are public record
like the blackened lung
in a cancer-society
advertisement: Don't.

*   *   *

I have another message.
This one's from Father: Goodbye.
Father, you didn't even try.

*   *   *

Now if you know who you are
you are the lucky one.
You other, we meet in this space,
there is nothing between us
but these pleasantries.
You see, I'm more Christian
than I imagined: In return for
your unkindnesses I give you
a kind of anonymous publicity.

*   *   *

And what is the fully developed
wrongheaded notion
really worth these days?

*   *   *

Some beautiful problems go unsolved
but are nevertheless celebrated.

Looking for Landmarks

For Bill

I took the path you said,
Brush up over my head,
Not to mention the night
Coming on full of clouds
And the way back forgotten.
I told myself
All real woes are personal
And therefore weatherable:
We make them public out
Of doubt or spite or to make
Certain they exist.

Doubtless, I said, this place
Is charted, and I could see
It checkered on the wall
With someone's positive pin
Stuck through it saying: Here.
You can do that
If you're important or
Arrogant enough.
But who was I? At some point
Lost, certain of nothing,
I had everything to learn.

The closer you get to things
The less you see of them,
I thought. I'm sure the spider
Doesn't think his web's
As perfect as we do.
To see our symmetry
It's better to try for distance,
But even then, walking
In circles you'll likely wind
Up a leaf over your head
For a roof and you smaller
Than anything.

I sat down under the devil's
Club, I picked the cobwebs
From my hands and eyes, and then
I saw so far down through
The trees my world flew back
To me and perched shimmering
In my eye. It stayed a moment
And then it was gone.
I moved on.

Spider

For days you dangle,
A speck in space,
The fine filaments
Of your web invisible
Against the off-white
Infinity of our living
Room. It is your sky,
A void in which you hang,
Sole citizen,
By day squeezing
Yourself squidlike
Into a narrow cotton tunnel
From which the beautiful
Geometry of your empty
City rays out into space.

At night you creep out
Thoughtfully to sun your-
Self in lamplight, trusting
In the chance event,
The accidental manna come
Bumbling into your world,
Shaking the streets,
An earthquake or skyquake

Bringing you scrambling
Like a true believer.
But nothing comes.
Each night after we have
Eaten, you hang above us
Like a famished question
Mark, so shy, so saintly and
Still, I cannot ignore you.

I catch a fly,
I place it in your web,
A buzzing breakfast
You will not eat.
You hide in your cave,
You peer at me like Plato's
Ghost, will none of my
Philanthropy.
The fly goes free,
While I sit here
Trying to understand
How the meek
Will ever inherit
Anything.

The Wars of Ambition

In the first scenario you pledge yourself
to an abstract Marxian dialectic—thesis,
antithesis, synthesis—guaranteed to work.
Off to the wars again, but the last stage
fails to materialize or the homemade bombs
explode on the way or the children
won't surrender, you surrender.

Then you try rhetoric: the classical schemes
which can't convince anyone much less
yourself, and the tropes—you become a ragman
peddling images of symbolic misfortune.
The furies tear you to pieces, and the wives.
Everyone examines you with the dispassionate
pity of a clinical psychiatrist.

Humility is the last temptation and the worst.
You break all your own windows and expect
to be praised if you can't be rewarded.
But the trouble is, everyone believes you.
You even believe you—it's your fault.
Then the cold creeps in and you run, you run
to stay warm, run for your life.

III

Four Fables

Owl

It is really a matter of geometry, said the owl.
Or, in Hardy's words, a convergence of the twain. I
track my shadow in the snow and where we meet we
eat. Yes, said the rabbit who had prudently armed
himself with a shotgun, and where my tracks end I
end. A pragmatic necessity, said the owl nervously
eyeing the shotgun. If I may interject a question,
said the snow, am I a historical record, or a tablecloth?

Porcupine

Defense is most important, said the porcupine,
I haven't the eagle's swiftness, the lion's courage,
the fox's cunning or the elephant's gravity. Yet,
like the best of scholars, I am capable of deep
penetration under pressure, and thus I obtain. But,
said the bobcat as he reached under the quilly cover
and flipped her on her back, you have no stomach
for it.

The Ice Dreams

At a certain time in my life I began to dream
of ice and avalanches. Always there was a far peak
cascading a glittering torrent of crystals which
became a river and then a valley and then a sea not
of water but of ice or snow. People always wondered
where it came from and I'd tell them: From the clouds,
where did you think? What clouds? they would ask.
Always the sky was clear, not a cloud in sight. Well
there *were* clouds, I'd say. Hmp! I'll bet, they'd
say and walk off. Always it was like that.

I got to making up stories: From the ice factory,
I'd say, from the weather bureau, from the
refrigerator. And they believed me. One day a whole
crowd of them ran past me shrieking, Help! Help!
What's the matter? I cried. It's the ice giant! one
said as he pattered past me over the snow. I thought
it might be a trick, or a truck. I could hear a distinct
rumbling. But no, it was the ice giant all right,
bringing us the inventory of icicles.

The Party

On the side of the mountain next to the glacier was a
little table where a mouse and three penguins were having a
tea party. Sugar or lemon? said one of the penguins. Both,
said the mouse. Neither, said one of the penguins. Sugar,
said the other. And the one who was serving put a twist of
lemon in his. Since it was the mouse's birthday tomorrow and
he wanted the penguins to know, he said, Tomorrow's my
birthday. Oh, said one of the penguins and sipped his tea
sedately. Isn't that nice! exclaimed another. But the third
frowned and said, I think it's dreadful! The others stared at
him speechless. The mouse started to reply but thought
better of it. For a long time nobody said anything. Finally,
the one who had spoken last said, as though to end the silence
which by now had become oppressive, Birthdays are really
a bore. They're supposed to make us happy, but really they
accomplish the opposite—they remind us we were born and
therefore we shall die. That's morbid, said the mouse. I
agree, said the second penguin. But the first said, in a tired
voice, Who cares? I mean really, if you're going to talk like
this you'll spoil the party. Which party? said the mouse, The
tea party or the birthday party?

IV

The Turkey-Quill Nymph

The turkey-quill nymph does not belong to that order
of semidivine beings imagined as beautiful maidens
inhabiting the sea, rivers, fountains, woods or trees
and said to attend upon the superior deities.
It is not a young and beautiful maiden, it has nothing
to do with the labia minora of the vulva or that genus
of aquatic plants which includes the common white
or yellow water lily and related species.

The turkey-quill nymph is tied on a size-fourteen hook,
or a size-sixteen when the water is gin clear, of spring
steel heavy enough to break the surface tension
of the water and sink to the required depth.
First, wrap the hook shank with one layer of thread
from the eye backwards to the throat.
Next, tie in the tail, a few wood-duck fibers,
and the body composed of one narrow strip
of dark turkey primary dressed with five turns
of fine brass wire. The shoulder may be tied
with two or three turns of peacock and the beard
with wood duck or, if you prefer, mallard.
Fish deep, casting as far out as possible,
letting the nymph sink to a count of twelve,
then work back in cautiously so
the curve of the line from rod tip to water is constant.

A strike may come swiftly,
burning the line from your fingers,
or as a barely perceptible change in the configuration
of the line as it lies atop the water,
in which case raise the rod firmly to set the hook
and pray that you've tied all your knots well.

These trout are large, by no means easy to land.
But should luck attend you, be sure to take no more
than you can eat, and put the rest back in the water,
holding them upright until they swim off
on their own power.

Davis Lake, Oregon

Georgic from Henry's Lake

It is like fishing for a line of poetry,
only in this case you already have the line
and the leader tied in diminishing lengths and strengths
and finished with the finest tippet.
The fly should be one of your own creation since
art is important here and the means of taking your trout
are as important as the end.

And, as in oratory, the presentation must be exact
lest you offend your audience, among whom the oldest
are invariably the wisest.
A line delivered too hastily will fall heavily,
driving away all but the most inexperienced and naïve.
Conversely, too casual an approach never reaches
its objective and may wind up in your head
or in a heap at your feet.
Sure coordination of the hand, eye and a
perfect sense of time are essential.
And finally, it helps to have balance.
This last is most important, for unless a universal
equanimity is created and sustained, any force will provoke
a counterforce to defeat you.

The object in this case is to roll the line
with enough impetus and finesse to duplicate nature,
so that the fly, mimicking its spent natural counterpart,
comes lightly and buoyantly to rest,
close enough to attract the attention of your quarry
but not so close as to frighten it.

If in addition to this you are patient,
content to endure long hours of painful reflection,
a shadow may rise swifter than thought
to shatter the blandest surface.
For ideas and trout strike when
least expected and are gone before we have grasped them.

But supposing for once you have done everything right,
and the barb is set,
the line must never be too tight lest the leader break
or the hook straighten.
On the other hand, if it is too slack the trout
may throw the fly on the first jump
or hang the line on a hidden snag.
As soon as possible you should retrieve all loose line,
especially if the fish runs toward you, playing it directly
from the reel, keeping the tackle at the proper angle
to avoid breaking it or using up its backbone,
thus losing all resilience
and in all likelihood the fish as well.
It will take at least this much skill and a little luck
to subdue your adversary
and much more self-discipline after it is safely landed
to let it go.

Henry's Lake, Idaho

Praise for the Saints in Time of War

There is no great art possible to a nation
but that which is based on battle
                                    —John Ruskin

The description of war as a means of protest,
the endless catalog of the abominable,
suffering depicted in minutest detail,
evil to be everywhere shunned but in art,
are not less revealing of one's true appetites
because adorned with righteousness.

In Van Honthorst's painting *Allegory of Vanity*
the eyes of Justice look deeply into ours,
the scales hang dead level from the left hand
while the right rests on the wooden frame
of a mirror reflecting the back of a human skull
resting on a closed book.

Followers of Loyola's spiritual disciplines
practiced nightly meditations by candlelight
in which they touched the eyeholes of that skull,
saw in the mirror their own eyes flicker and go out.
Prayer and fasting brought to such a pitch
death the hand could see and eyes touch.

The lives of saints are incomprehensible to us
who in our weakness despair of attaining perfection:
Imponderable rectitude beyond all human enterprise,
beyond even the vanity of poetry—we can but honor it.
Yet is it because we can't stand an artlessness
beyond gambit and mate we fiddle with words,

throats choked with the burnt odors of conquest?
If there is anything honorable in our work
we should be the last to know, our best hope
the possibility that stubbornness may trick us
by accident into truthfulness—as in, for example,
Vignon's *Martyrdom of St. Matthew*, the blood

escaping along the sword blade,
less mortifying than that bemused
imbecility of the assassin's face.

Endurances

A mountain climber turned evangelist confesses,
"Hanging on a face, I think like a fly.
The slightest error will kill.
And when I'm so close to death
suddenly I think of life.
The lichen in the crevices burns
with a pale green flame,
I think with my fingertips and toes,
no ideas but what I see and touch.
I think of Lot's wife and don't look back."

A sociologist tells of a soldier
squatting by the roadside after an ambush
in which two of his friends had been killed,
weeping, rapt over the simple beauty of a flower,
the meaning of which was surely lost
on the objective detachment of the unbiased observer
who could but wonder at the absurd juxtaposition,
the blood in the ditches and the blood-red flower.

I have heard a racing driver tell of hurling his
life through sudden turns so fast
he lost himself in stillness,
became a cipher on the tachometer,
the blurred shape of a bird in a dream of trees.

And diving we find a rapture in the depths,
when perceiving our immortality we tear off masks
and glide naked and glistening to our deaths.

V

Narcissus: A Notebook

i

When I woke it was spring,
rain fell from the eaves,
in the night
first squadrons of geese
flew north.
All quarter I had cursed
the dullness of my students—
and forgiven my own.
That sensibility responsive
to the least echo,
where was it?

This morning they've repaid my unkindness
with two daffodils in a tall jar.
While they write and chew their pencils
I study each six-petaled blossom
with a bundle of anthers
in its blue-green opening,
a black spot like the eye of a snail
on every filament surrounding
the trefoil-tipped pistil,
head bowing shyly from its stem,
the fluted edge of the bell,
the six pointed papery petals
bright butter yellow tinged with green.

Daffodil, narcissus, asphodel, Williams' flower,
flower of the fields
where the shades of dead heroes wander,
yellow flower growing at the brink of
the deep pool with its eye like a mirror,
poor flower, in April blossoming in rain,
stalk broken by hail, face down,
petals muddied and crushed like Ophelia's petticoats,
narcissus,
in most regions of the West most valuable
of the spring-flowering bulbous plants,
permanent, increasing yearly, hardy to cold and heat,
scorned by the gopher, loved by the snail.

The leaves are flat and strap-shaped or narrow like rushes,
the flowers basic yellows and whites, oranges and reds,
or apricots, pinks and creams.

ii

Was this the secret I had looked for and forgotten—
the sixfold present golden genius—
while peering out the window through venetian blinds
getting dust on my nose, absent-minded, laughable,
walking around more and more with hands in my pockets?

Wednesday, April 7, 11:45, eye checkup.

A more important lesson: Light is the life of man,
the eye is the light of the body.

To know thoroughly a particular reality:
Can we intuit others from it?
Every intuition is a gamble.
Consider the lilies of the field:
Are you merely a magnetic field
of spinning atoms and electrons,
Einstein's photons,
when your scent fills me with joy?

When the light is made to move in a circle
all the energies of heaven and earth,
of the light and the dark, are crystallized . . .
the light flower of heaven and earth
fills all the thousand spaces.

Writing 313: Observe immediate concrete objects—
a flower, a stone, a leaf, running water, a face,
hands, feet, the folds in clothing;
try following with the eye every branch, every twist
and turn of a tree from the trunk to the tip
of the topmost limb—the eye as squirrel.

Student paper: "Man must attempt something he considers
crucial before he becomes at peace with himself."

the world shall know us by our works,
the gods by these pencil chewings, mutterings,
discarded drafts and faults.

> Last night I dreamed I found
> in the bottom of an old chest
> a beautiful book of poems
> written by my kind
> but unliterate stepfather.

iii

Midway between the hugest red star, the smallest electron,
I can't turn my eyes from this world and don't want to.
Flowers and novas, snowflakes and diatoms,
observable and immeasurable explosions of species,
brief love affairs and words confuse me,
looking for order with a mind in chaos,
considering all the physical evidence of a fear,
letting the light fall past my hearing,
letting the eye mislead the eye.

That afternoon we walked through the badlands
and saw the earth forgetting itself
and believed in those scars,
believed weather might reveal us.

And in the Wind River Canyon
in a lightning storm
we saw the same colors
only this time more intense,
and stopping to look
found a red-shafted flicker
trapped in a ball of line,
with a fishhook through its leg.
Together we held it
and cut the hook free,
then watched it fly off
between lightning breaks.

Coming back from the river
where I'd washed the blood
from my hands
I found the dried remains
of a young kingfisher,
ants crawling from its eyesockets,
and didn't tell you.
That night in the Tetons
I lay awake
with my hands over my eyes.
Clouds filled all the mountains.

iv

After they had prepared his funeral pyre
they turned and found where his body had been
a flower of gold with white-brimmed petals.
Narcissus, Narcissus, we are what we long for.
Now you are everywhere in spring,
under trees and flowering shrubs,
among ground-cover plantings,
near water, in rock gardens and patios
or in borders by secret pathways
or naturalized in sweeping drifts
wherever light and space are available.